ISO 9001 & I

Rethinking Solutions

Dennis McVay

ISO 9001 & PPAP

Rethinking Solutions

www.JustRethink.com

ISO 9001 & PPAP - Rethinking Solutions

This book is dedicated to those

who have still not given up on

finding the **KEY** to success!

This work is copyrighted © 2017. All rights reserved. No part of this publication may be reproduced or distributed in any form without the prior written permission from JUSTRETHINK, LLC.

About the Author

Dennis McVay is the CEO of JUSTRETHINK, LLC and has over 24 years of hands-on industry experience working and consulting for small companies to extremely large tier one automotive suppliers.

McVay has a proven track record as an advanced problem solver with degrees, certifications and expertise in Design Engineering, Manufacturing, Quality Engineering, Automation & Robotics, Senior Level IT Analyst & Programming, Safety and Senior Level Management.

McVay leads by example, working through complex problems, by taking a unique, common sense approach offering time-saving teaching mechanisms.

McVay knows how to make things simple for others to understand. The Rethinking Solutions book word counts are designed to be less than a one hour read.

McVay is excited to share real world "hands-on" solutions to you through these new Rethinking Solutions Books and Android Phone APPs.

Table of Contents

Introduction 6

Plan for Success 10

Synergy Self-Assessment 12

Employee Satisfaction 13

OSHA & Safety 14

How to Merge PPAP into ISO 9001 18

ISO 9001 & PPAP 21

Receiving Quality Materials 49

Supplier Corrective Action Request (SCAR) 50

Conclusion 51

Review Questions 53

Index 54

ISO 9001 & PPAP - Rethinking Solutions

Introduction

At JUSTRETHINK, LLC we speak plain English when it comes to solving complex problems.

Rethink by definition is to think again about something, in order to change it for the better.

So, before we look at outside suppliers and the ISO TS16949 Production, Part, Approval, Process (PPAP) and how to integrate with the ISO 9001:2015 standard, let's take a moment to do a basic self-assessment.

Let's review, after WWII a management expert tried to help our U.S. manufacturing, but nobody would listen. Why? Because he could prove that most defects were caused from the shortcomings of poor management and not from workers being set up for failure.

Poor management? How could this be, what do you mean? I have an impressive degree from an elite university, a Six-Sigma Black Belt, and many years of experience managing people.

Sorry to be the one to tell you, but if you are failing daily to keep your best employees, customers and EBITDA's (Earnings Before Interest, Taxes, Depreciation and Amortization) satisfied, then none of your credentials matter. Good news! JUSTRETHINK, LLC can help.

ISO 9001 & PPAP - Rethinking Solutions

We have studied the experts and have read many leather-bound books on ISO Standards, Quality, LEAN, Six-Sigma, Auditing, Leadership, Manufacturing and Management. We have encountered many "know-it-all" professionals, some with impressive degrees from universities we did not have the privilege to attend, and yet they are "quality clueless" when it comes to solving hands-on factory production challenges.

Unplug from your meetings, quit drowning in the negative data and stop assuming your highly paid leadership team has a magic wand that can be used every time things go south, fix this Deja vu and take the BS by the horns and ask yourself… Can I actually build the products to the quality levels I expect from my employees, with the tools and materials I have provided them? Seriously Rethink about that for a minute.

We challenge you to start leading by example. Gear up with the proper Personal Protective Equipment (PPE), go out to the shop floor and work station by work station until the product is shipped.

Then visit your customer service department to call the customer and verify that the packaging protected the unit being shipped and that they are 100% satisfied.

ISO 9001 & PPAP - Rethinking Solutions

Unfortunately, unless you are in the food or pharmaceutical industries, this is what we typically find at most manufacturing companies:

- Work instructions missing or incomplete
- Equipment in poor shape
- No Preventative Maintenance (PM) records
- Safety violations [Including Material Safety Data Sheets (MSDS)]
- Calibration violations
- Workstations unorganized (Missing Poka-Yoke, 5s, LEAN, etc.)
- Operator's Training Matrix not accurate or using undocumented Tribal Knowledge
- Operator does not know the company's Quality or Mission Statement
- Language barriers, some operators cannot speak or read English
- Engineering design flaws and poor relational tolerances
- Technology working against production
- Equipment not fit for the intended use and cannot run at rates
- Poor supervision. For example, go out to the shop unannounced and start working where you normally would not be and wait. A good supervisor should be alert and immediately question your intentions and/or offer training and to help right away. What did you discover?

Also, now is a good time to practice active listening. While you are on the plant floor, take time to interact with the employees at the bottom, shake people's hands to earn their trust. We all enjoy verbal recognition from time to time and basic respect goes a long way.

If you are a new manager hired to fix years of chaos plant wide, I would strongly advise hiring an outside consultant to do some anonymous surveys and evaluations. I know for a fact, that not all managers or supervisors can lead people and that most good employees will give up on making their boss look good and start seeking other employment opportunities. Why? Negativity creates negativity, which leads to drama.

If you took the challenge above, you now know that boots on the ground is the answer. Lead by example and remember, satisfied employees create satisfied customers by working with you and not against you.

You may have to reorganize your team, but once you get the basic manufacturing and management systems working, plug ISO 9001:2015 back in and apply PPAP to get control of your Quality Management System (QMS) and supplier quality.

Remember garbage in, garbage out!

JUSTRETHINK is here to teach you how to make the advanced automotive PPAP work inside a smaller ISO 9001:2015 system, while applying teaching mechanisms to help non-ISO companies learn to train to contain through Supplier Corrective Action Requests (SCARs).

Onward!

Plan for Success

Before we go any further, let's plan for success.

To be blunt, if you do not have authority to make changes from the top down to the Quality Department, update your resume and move on. We have been there and done that and, unfortunately, it is the cold hard truth.

Again, if your organizational chart does not put the QUALITY Department above all other groups, then you do not have the authority to encourage or motivate others to do their jobs, especially when people fear change.

Quality auditors do one thing very well, we find fault in other people's work, which by design, will upset most, but for the greater good of the company and customer satisfaction.

ISO 9001 & PPAP - Rethinking Solutions

So yes, it will eventually happen, that a conflict of interest occurs that ultimately compromises the production quality system. Let's assume Quality finds a key engineering design flaw at the last minute, but there is a deadline to ship. The plant manager uses authority above Quality, to issue a deviation request to overrule, so the product (regardless of quality) is shipped on time. Now you have a weak or careless Quality Department.

Speaking of quality audits, do you cringe every time you hear the word audit? Do you spend more time coaching your employees on what to say, what to do and how to act while you are being audited, do you play games with the auditor, so they will not discover your closet full of violations?

If you said YES, stop playing the audit games that makes your ISO 9001 certification a sales tool and get back to the basics of doing things right the first time, documenting what you do and then doing what you have documented. You control the documentation, so make things audit friendly.

This book assumes your company has a working ISO 9001:2015 wanting to incorporate PPAP solutions to help eliminate supplier risks. In order to keep you on the plan for success, you will need some synergy.

ISO 9001 & PPAP - Rethinking Solutions

Synergy Self-Assessment

A successful business must create quality products at an affordable price, with on-time delivery… Agree?

To do this you need Synergy between ALL departments:

- All Management Teams
- Design Engineers
- Manufacturing Engineers
- Material Suppliers
- Quality Teams
- Marketing Teams
- Sales Teams
- Supervisors and Line Leads
- Production Employees
- Distribution
- Customer Relations
- OTHERS

Without satisfied employees working together as a team, being successful in producing quality products will be potluck.

Good news. This is fixable, so let's Just Rethink employee satisfaction

Employee Satisfaction

- ✓ Satisfied employees, create satisfied customers
- ✓ Satisfied employees, go above and beyond to make the goals
- ✓ Satisfied employees, come in early and work late
- ✓ Satisfied employees, are brand loyal and promote sales
- ✓ Satisfied employees, will coach others to success
- ✓ Satisfied employees, will lead by example
- ✓ Satisfied employees, work with you and not against you
- ✓ Satisfied employees, help achieve production goals
- ✓ Satisfied employees, voice alerts to make things better
- ✓ Satisfied employees, help pass ISO 9001 audits
- ✓ Satisfied employees, police the Quality Management System
- ✓ Satisfied employees, identify problems quicker with experience
- ✓ Satisfied employees, care about safety and wearing PPE
- ✓ Satisfied employees, won't become disgruntled whistleblowers
- ✓ Satisfied employees, helps with housekeeping, LEAN & 5s
- ✓ Satisfied employees, are dependable and predictable
- ✓ Satisfied employees, _____

We all know money is the ultimate motivator, but recognitions, donuts, gift cards, bonuses, and respect go a long way. I once worked for a company that made everyone wear the same company logo shirts, yes even the CEO looked the same as the janitor, just to illustrate how everyone was equally important. No matter what you do, just make work fun again.

There are pros and cons in everything we do, eliminate the headaches to justify satisfaction rewards. Without good, well trained and satisfied employees, what kind of quality would you be willing to predict?

ISO 9001 & PPAP - Rethinking Solutions

OSHA & Safety

Okay, now that we have a team of satisfied employees, let's keep them safe and free of injuries. This book is not intended to be a safety manual, but I must point out a few KEY reminders that you should Just Rethink.

- ✓ Do you know the Occupational Safety and Health Administration (OSHA.gov) by law requires that employers provide their employees with safe working conditions?

- ✓ Do you know a fatality accident must be reported to OSHA within 8-hours and all other serious injuries within 24 hours?

- ✓ Do you know that over 2 billion employees have smartphones with cameras and are protected by the whistleblower act?

- ✓ If you have 5 minutes to prove evidence to an OSHA Inspector, would you Pass or Fail?

- ✓ Does your Training Matrix match what the employee actually remembers or currently knows about safety?

- ✓ Does your employee know that MSDS stands for Material Safety Data Sheet and are they able to take you to the actual reference manual location and then look up the chemical in question and explain the first aid instructions without hesitation or assistance?

- ✓ Does the employee know to never use a chemical without a proper label and what is the correct PPE to wear?

ISO 9001 & PPAP - Rethinking Solutions

- ✓ Does the employee understand chemical labels? Labels tell you what the chemical is, who made it, why or if it is dangerous and how to protect yourself.

- ✓ Does the employee know how to read the National Fire Protection Association (NFPA.org) color coded labels and number system?
    - o Red means fire hazard and the number states how bad
    - o Yellow means reactivity hazard (Don't mix with other chemicals)
    - o Blue means a health hazard
    - o White means specific hazard or PPE requirements

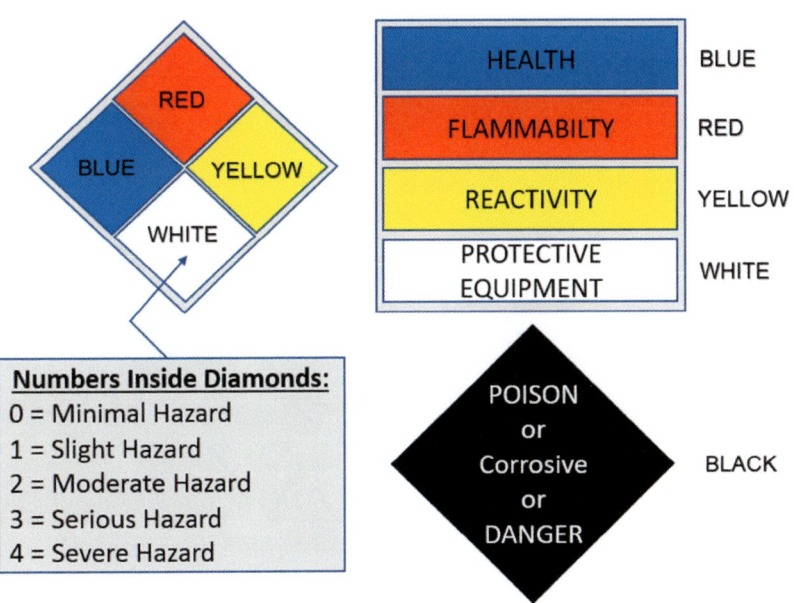

KEY NOTE: Employees have a legal "Right to Know" about chemical hazards.

ISO 9001 & PPAP - Rethinking Solutions

- ✓ Do your employees have hands-on fire extinguisher training or other control measures/emergency training in the event something goes terribly wrong?

- ✓ Do you have building alarms for fire, tornado or other alerts to assist employees or visitors with one or multiple disabilities?

- ✓ Do you know bloodborne pathogens are seriously infectious and can cause diseases in humans, like Hepatitis B & C, HIV and that OSHA requires you to have a certified trained employee for blood cleanup?

- ✓ Do you know how much blood will be hazardously shared, before first aid for a minor finger cut can be found?

- ✓ Do you know who is going to clean up the blood trail created along the way and where they will properly dispose of all the blood covered hazardous waste?

- ✓ Get your employee's trained and OSHA certified to stay healthy!

- ✓ Do you have a dress code to prevent long hair and loose clothing from becoming an injury around certain rotating machines?

- ✓ Do you have a clean safe work environment?

- ✓ Do not overlook safety, while doing quality audits! Do your part to work smart. Safety should not be found by accident.

ISO 9001 & PPAP - Rethinking Solutions

We just covered a few KEY examples to help you "Rethink" Employee Satisfaction and Safety. Keep in mind, every company will have safety issues. Some might be caused by an unexpected roof leak, a damaged machine guard, somebody not wearing PPE and/or not following Standard Work Instructions (SWI) or OSHA's required lock out, tag out.

Either way, safe satisfied employees with proper training will go above and beyond to help police these issues to keep more focus on producing quality products for your satisfied customers, with less downtime.

Just Rethink ISO 9001 for a minute. The typical business case for ISO 9001 was to enhance world trade. In other words, ISO 9001 controls the quality standards, so multiple ISO 9001 certified companies can compete to make the exact same part for one customer. If everyone follows the ISO 9001 quality standards, the purchased parts are truly universal at the highest quality levels. If you are not ISO 9001 Certified, you cannot bid on various contracts. However, if your products are stand alone and not required as a mating part for another customer's assembly, then the ISO 9001 Certification gives you no sales advantage for contract bidding. ISO 9001 Certification tells the world that your company offers proof of performance and accountability at all levels of the operation to achieve quality excellence. However, you should already have a strong, quality-focused manufacturing foundation in place, before attempting to purchase ISO 9001 and or adding PPAP. ISO 9001 promotes "Continuous Improvement", so make sure you fix the basic improvements before merging more standards and regulations into the mix.

ISO 9001 & PPAP - Rethinking Solutions

How to Merge PPAP into ISO 9001

Next, we need to add the proper language to merge PPAP into your existing Quality Management System (QMS). To do this navigate to your appropriate ISO 9001:2015 sections below and apply suggested updates.

- ✓ ISO 9001:2015 Section 4.4 – Quality management system and its processes:
    - ○ UPDATE Revision level to include these new PPAP additions.

    - ○ ADD to DEFINITION Section:
        - ▪ PPAP = Production Parts Approval Process

    - ○ ADD to REFERENCE Section:
        - ▪ PPAP Documents [See Sample Illustrations 1-2 & 2-1]

    - ○ ADD to RESPONSIBILITY Section:
        - ▪ Supplier quality manager is responsible for PPAP

    - ○ UPDATE Section 6.3 - Planning of changes:
        - ▪ UPDATE Flowcharts to logically include PPAP

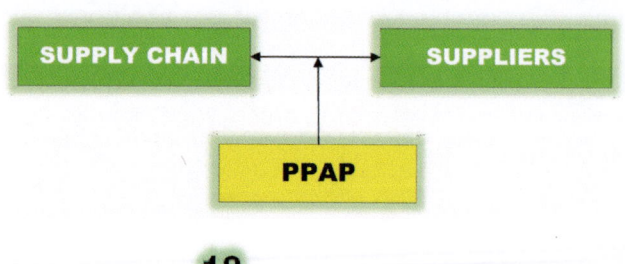

- UPDATE Section 8.4.1 – General under Section header 8.4 Control of externally provided processes, products and services:
  - ADD this language: "PPAP is required anytime a new part or a change to an existing part or process is being planned. It is at the discretion of <YOUR COMPANY NAME> to determine when or if a PPAP submission will be required."

- UPDATE Section 8.4.3 – Information for external providers
  - ADD this language: "As a supplier you should have the type of quality system that develops all of the requirements of a PPAP submission regardless of whether or not you have been asked to deliver a PPAP submission. <YOUR COMPANY NAME> assumes a good faith agreement with each supplier with respect to change management. Therefore, <YOUR COMPANY NAME> relies on each Supplier to notify us if anything planned or unplanned occurs that could affect the quality of the part or service being provided to <YOUR COMPANY NAME>. In the event a PPAP submission is not requested, <YOUR COMPANY NAME> reserves the right to request any of these documents at any time during the life of the product. In the event of a supplier nonconformance, a Supplier Corrective Action Request (SCAR) will be issued for cost

ISO 9001 & PPAP - Rethinking Solutions

recovery, which includes materials, labor, etc. and all consequential damages."

- UPDATE Section 7.5.3.2 – Control of documented information
  - ADD this language: "Documents, master sample and PPAP sample parts associated with Production Parts Approval Process (PPAP) signed warrant should be maintained for life of production plus one year."

KEY NOTE: If your QMS policy is divided out into many separate individual documents, you will need to duplicate this logic and language throughout by possibly adding the word "PPAP" and a few tweaks here and there to make everything read well and apply to your specific industry.

Congratulations, you have just merged the PPAP language into your ISO 9001's Quality Management System.

Next, we need to create the actual PPAP warrant package documents and add to them to your existing controlled document reference section. These will be the PPAP forms you send to your suppliers.

ISO 9001 & PPAP

Production Part Approval Process (PPAP) was developed within the Automotive Industry Action Group (AIAG.org) in Michigan around 1982.

PPAP is a detailed supplier quality template that covers all the advanced requirements for the complex manufacturing of precision applications.

The goal of this book is how to adapt the wonderful world of PPAP to meet smaller, less complex projects found in the world of ISO 9001:2015 vs ISO TS 16949 standards. You know - the suppliers not manufacturing automobiles, airplanes, etc. or space ships.

The PPAP process ensures that all designs and specifications are understood by the supplier, so your production will consistently run at rate, with no interruptions. PPAP is your solution to get it right from the start.

We all know that you cannot keep your customers satisfied, without using quality suppliers, so let me explain how PPAP works. Typically, a project manager within your company will require either a "New Product", "Engineering Change" to an existing item or there may be a "Supplier Initiated Change" and/or something labeled "Other" as required. When this happens, a supplier will be contacted by the project manager and will requests samples for your companies engineering department to review for fit, form and function. The PPAP submittal starts after these samples pass Design Failure Mode Effect Analysis (DFMEA), Process Failure Mode Effect

ISO 9001 & PPAP - Rethinking Solutions

Analysis (PFMEA) to get Engineering Change Number (ECN) and management's final approval.

Yes! PPAP comes last, before the purchase order is approved. The project manager will be responsible for gathering and submitting information as required for the PPAP.

The project manager's duties include:

- ✓ Gathering and labeling the approved engineering sample as the "Master" sample with the approval date.

- ✓ Complete the initial PPAP document:
    - PPAP Number
    - Supplier Code
    - Requestor's Name
    - Location/Division
    - Part Name
    - Part Number
    - Drawing Number
    - Drawing Revision Date
    - Supplier Status
    - Reason for Submission
    - PPAP Level 1, 2, 3, 4 or 5 as required
    - Number of PPAP samples required for the submittal
    - The project manager will send the initialized PPAP, typically a spreadsheet with organized tabs, to the supplier for them to finish filling in all the blanks and to import photo evidence as required

- o The deadline for the returned PPAP submittal and sample parts is up to the project manager.
- o Once the PPAP document and sample parts are returned, the project manager will deliver, along with Engineering's master sample to the supplier quality manager for review.
- o The project manager, must wait for the supplier quality manager's approval, before issuing the purchase order to purchase these products for production.
- o Once the project manager obtains the purchase order number, they must update the original PPAP "Purchase Order Number" field to finish the approved PPAP signed warrant.

Let us now take a closer look at a sample PPAP submission package cover page example (*See Illustration 1-1*) Please note this is one example of a custom form. You will need to create your own to include the company logo, etc. and then formulate the menus for auto completion, add various tabs for the evidence you require and color code for mistake proofing (Poka-Yoke) to achieve your exact PPAP requirements.

KEY NOTE: Don't let the PPAP package creation process overwhelm you. All of this paper work is designed to cover these basic goals:

1. Verify Engineering's master sample, matches the PPAP samples
2. Verify all of the PPAP paperwork was completed correctly
3. Verify all the evidence collected is good for production
4. Prevent nonconforming materials from being shipped to you

ISO 9001 & PPAP - Rethinking Solutions

Our sample cover form (*See Illustration 1-1*) has fill in the blanks, laid out as follows for your reference;

- ✓ PPAP # [This will be the next sequential number you pick from a custom PPAP sequential number spreadsheet log. If you don't have a sequential number log, create one inside your favorite spreadsheet software to track and prevent duplicate PPAP Numbers.]

- ✓ PURCHASE ORDER NUMBER: [This gets completed last, after the Supplier quality manager approves PPAP]

- ✓ REQUESTOR: [This is the Project manager's Name]

- ✓ TYPE OF PPAP - CHECK BOXES: [Select One]
    - o NEW PRODUCT?
    - o ENGINEERING CHANGE?
    - o SUPPLIER INITIATED CHANGE?
    - o OTHER?

- ✓ PART NAME: [See your engineering's drawing and enter the Part Name]

- ✓ PART NUMBER: [See your engineering's drawing and enter the Part Number]

- ✓ DRAWING NUMBER: [See your engineering's drawing and enter the Drawing Number]

- ✓ DRAWING REVISION DATE: [See your engineering's drawing and enter the Drawings Revision Date]

ISO 9001 & PPAP - Rethinking Solutions

KEY NOTE: If for some reason, your engineering department does not have a drawing, take the entire supplier's drawing with title block and tolerances and do a screen clip and then cut and paste this on to your title block with a disclaimer that supplier's title block supersedes your company's title block. Save with your new drawing number and your part number. This will give you a quick drawing and keep all the risk on the supplier's drawing.

- ✓ SUPPLIER PART NAME: [See supplier's drawing and enter the Supplier Part Name]

- ✓ SUPPLIER PART NUMBER: [See supplier's drawing and enter the Supplier Part Number]

- ✓ SUPPLIER DRAWING NUMBER: [See supplier's drawing and enter the Supplier Drawing Number]

- ✓ SUPPLIER DRAWING REVISION DATE: [See supplier's drawing and enter the Supplier Drawings Revision Date]

- ✓ CERTIFICATIONS (WHERE REQUIRED): [Some industries may require parts to pass various certifications – list here]

- ✓ CERTIFICATIONS (WHERE REQUIRED) RENEWAL DATE: [Some industries may require parts to pass various certifications. These certifications will have an expiration date – list here]

ISO 9001 & PPAP - Rethinking Solutions

- ✓ MATERIAL CERTIFICATION NUMBER: [Some materials will have a certified mill test report or an inspection certificate that states a materials chemical and physical properties complies with ISO / ANSI / ASME specific standards. Enter this here]

- ✓ MATERIAL CERTIFICATION NUMBERS MFG DATE: [Enter certified report date here]

- ✓ SUPPLIER BUSINESS NAME: [Enter supplier's name]

- ✓ SUPPLIER CODE: [Suppliers must be approved per evaluations listed in ISO 9001:2015 Section 8.4 – Approved suppliers will have code assigned to them from accounting – Enter it here]

- ✓ SUPPLIER STREET ADDRESS: [Enter supplier's street address]

- ✓ SUPPLIER CITY/STATE/ZIP: [Enter supplier's city, state and zip]

- ✓ SUPPLIER CONTACT NAME: [Enter supplier's contact name]

- ✓ LOCATION / DIVISION: [This is your company's location/division – sometimes a plant will operate in various locations or divisions – Enter it here]

- ✓ SOURCING MANAGER: [This is your company's sourcing manager and in most cases, this might be the same as the project manager]

- ✓ OTHER: [This is an extra field for other information]

ISO 9001 & PPAP - Rethinking Solutions

- ✓ ORIGINAL MANUFACTURER INFORMATION: [This section is to be used when the supplier purchases the part from another manufacturer and sells it back to your company]

    - o FACTORY NAME: [Name of 3rd party supplier]
    - o VENDOR CODE: [This is the supplier's code to track this 3rd party supplier]
    - o STREET ADDRESS: [Enter 3rd party supplier's street address]
    - o CITY/STATE/ZIP: [Enter 3rd party supplier's city, state and zip]
    - o CONTACT NAME: [Enter 3rd party supplier's contact name]
    - o LOCATION / DIVISION: [This is the 3rd party's location/division]
    - o SOURCING MANAGER: [This is the supplier's sourcing manager that is purchasing form the 3rd party supplier]
    - o OTHER: [This is an extra field for other information]

- ✓ SUPPLIER STATUS - CHECK BOXES: [Select YES or NO]
    - o Is the Supplier New or Existing?
        - ▪ YES or NO
    - o If NEW, has the Supplier Selection & Approval process been initiated?
        - ▪ YES or NO

- ✓ REASON FOR SUBMISSION - CHECK BOXES: [Select One]
    - o New Component / Initial Submission
    - o New Supplier for Existing Component
    - o Supplier initiated changes that affect Form, Fit or Function

ISO 9001 & PPAP - Rethinking Solutions

- o Existing component that has NOT been purchased for + 2 years
- o Engineering Change
- o Tooling: Transfer, Replacement, Refurbishment or Additional
- o Change to Optional Construction or Material
- o Part Produced at Additional Location
- o Sub-Supplier or Material Source Change
- o OTHER: Please Specify Reason(s) Below
  - REASON(S) = [Data Entry Lines]

✓ VENDOR REQUESTED SUBMITTAL - CHECK BOXES: [Select one of the five PPAP Warrant levels explained below based on your detailed requirements.]

- o **LEVEL 1** – PART SUBMISSION WARRANT (PSW)
  - PPAP Submission Checklist #13 – Appearance Approval Report (AAR)
  - PPAP Submission Checklist #18 – Part Submission Warrant (PSW), which is your entire PPAP submittal
  - **KEY NOTE:** Rarely used, but available

- o **LEVEL 2** – PART SUBMISSION WARRANT (PSW) WITH PRODUCT SAMPLES AND LIMITED SUPPORTING DATA
  - PPAP Submission Checklist #1 – Design Documentation
  - PPAP Submission Checklist #2 – Engineering Change Documents
  - PPAP Submission Checklist #9 – Dimensional Analysis
  - PPAP Submission Checklist #10 – Initial Sample Inspection Report

- PPAP Submission Checklist #12 – Qualified Laboratory Documentation
- PPAP Submission Checklist #13 – Appearance Approval Report (AAR)
- PPAP Submission Checklist #14 – Sample Production Parts
- PPAP Submission Checklist #18 – Part Submission Warrant (PSW), which is your entire PPAP submittal
- **KEY NOTE:** Used as needed

○ **LEVEL 3** – PART SUBMISSION WARRANT (PSW) WITH PRODUCT SAMPLES AND COMPLETE SUPPORTING DATA
- PPAP Submission Checklist #1 – Design Documentation
- PPAP Submission Checklist #2 – Engineering Change Documents
- PPAP Submission Checklist #3 – Engineering Approval
- PPAP Submission Checklist #4 – Design Failure Mode Effect Analysis (DFMEA)
- PPAP Submission Checklist #5 – Process Flow Diagram
- PPAP Submission Checklist #6 – Process Failure Mode Effect Analysis (PFMEA)
- PPAP Submission Checklist #7 – Control Plan
- PPAP Submission Checklist #8 – Measurement System Analysis (MSA)
- PPAP Submission Checklist #9 – Dimensional Analysis

ISO 9001 & PPAP - Rethinking Solutions

- PPAP Submission Checklist #10 – Initial Sample Inspection Report
- PPAP Submission Checklist #11 – Initial Process Studies
- PPAP Submission Checklist #12 – Qualified Laboratory Documentation
- PPAP Submission Checklist #13 – Appearance Approval Report (AAR)
- PPAP Submission Checklist #14 – Sample Production Parts
- PPAP Submission Checklist #17– Records Material / Performance Tests
- PPAP Submission Checklist #18– Part Submission Warrant (PSW), which is your entire PPAP submittal
- **KEY NOTE:** Used daily

  - **LEVEL 4** – PART SUBMISSION WARRANT (PSW) AND OTHER SPECIAL REQUIREMENTS AS DEFINED
    - PPAP Submission Checklist #1 – Design Documentation
    - PPAP Submission Checklist #2 – Engineering Change Documents
    - PPAP Submission Checklist #3 – Engineering Approval
    - PPAP Submission Checklist #4 – Design Failure Mode Effect Analysis (DFMEA)
    - PPAP Submission Checklist #5 – Process Flow Diagram
    - PPAP Submission Checklist #6 – Process Failure Mode Effect Analysis (PFMEA)
    - PPAP Submission Checklist #7 – Control Plan

- PPAP Submission Checklist #8 – Measurement System Analysis (MSA)
- PPAP Submission Checklist #9 – Dimensional Analysis
- PPAP Submission Checklist #10 – Initial Sample Inspection Report
- PPAP Submission Checklist #11 – Initial Process Studies
- PPAP Submission Checklist #12 – Qualified Laboratory Documentation
- PPAP Submission Checklist #13 – Appearance Approval Report (AAR)
- PPAP Submission Checklist #14 – Sample Production Parts
- PPAP Submission Checklist #15 – Master Sample
- PPAP Submission Checklist #16 – Checking Aids
- PPAP Submission Checklist #17 – Records Material / Performance Tests
- PPAP Submission Checklist #18 – Part Submission Warrant (PSW), which is your entire PPAP submittal
- **KEY NOTE:** Rarely used

- **LEVEL 5** – VISIT MANUFACTURING LOCATION FOR AUDIT / INSPECTION: THIS INCLUDES EVERYTHING WITHIN SUBMISSION LEVELS 1 THRU 4
    - PPAP Submission Checklist #1 – Design Documentation
    - PPAP Submission Checklist #2 – Engineering Change Documents
    - PPAP Submission Checklist #3 – Engineering Approval

ISO 9001 & PPAP - Rethinking Solutions

- PPAP Submission Checklist #4 – Design Failure Mode Effect Analysis (DFMEA)
- PPAP Submission Checklist #5 – Process Flow Diagram
- PPAP Submission Checklist #6 – Process Failure Mode Effect Analysis (PFMEA)
- PPAP Submission Checklist #7 – Control Plan
- PPAP Submission Checklist #8 – Measurement System Analysis (MSA)
- PPAP Submission Checklist #9 – Dimensional Analysis
- PPAP Submission Checklist #10 – Initial Sample Inspection Report
- PPAP Submission Checklist #11 – Initial Process Studies
- PPAP Submission Checklist #12 – Qualified Laboratory Documentation
- PPAP Submission Checklist #13 – Appearance Approval Report (AAR)
- PPAP Submission Checklist #14 – Sample Production Parts
- PPAP Submission Checklist #15 – Master Sample
- PPAP Submission Checklist #16 – Checking Aids
- PPAP Submission Checklist #17– Records Material / Performance Tests
- PPAP Submission Checklist #18– Part Submission Warrant (PSW), which is your entire PPAP submittal
- **KEY NOTE:** Used when you need a full audit on-site

✓ DISCLAIMERS: [Add your special requirements here]

- o All samples submitted must be tagged and identified appropriately. Please print and attach our provided shipping label.
- o Prior to PPAP submittal, all Critical To Quality (CtQ's) must meet or exceed a Process Capability Index (CpK) of 1.33 and ALL dimensions (including dimensions not identified as critical to quality) must fall within specifications of drawing.

✓ DECLARATION = [Fill in blanks as required]
- o LEGAL STATEMENT: [I hereby affirm that the samples represented by this warrant are representative of standard production and that all submission meet requirements as well as all other applicable regulatory standards and specifications.]

KEY NOTE: In the automotive world, PPAP's can cost a lot of money for traveling, RUN at RATE verifications, etc. and most likely negotiated inside the purchase order up front... but when you don't have the budget to dive that deep and you want the security of PPAP, then you have to address and input these types of legal statements. I would also tighten the belt on your ISO 9001 Supplier Risk Assessments.

- o NAME: [Supplier's Name]
- o TITLE: [Supplier's Company Title]
- o PHONE: [Supplier's Phone]
- o FAX: [Supplier's Fax]
- o E-MAIL: [Supplier's E-mail]
- o DATE: [Date Supplier Signed]

- PPAP APPROVAL SIGNATURE: [This is the Supplier quality manager's signature and is completed once everything is approved for production]

KEY NOTE: Don't forget to make this a controlled document with a revision date. Congratulations, you just completed a PPAP Submission Cover Sheet.

ISO 9001 & PPAP - Rethinking Solutions

Production Part Approval Process(PPAP) SUBMISSION PACKAGE COVER

PPAP #: _____ Purchase Order Number: _____ REQUESTOR: _____

☐ NEW PRODUCT ☐ ENGINEERING CHANGE ☐ SUPPLIER INITIATED CHANGE ☐ OTHER

PART INFORMATION:
- Part Name: _____
- Part Number: _____
- Drawing Number: _____ Revision Date: _____
- Supplier Part Name: _____
- Supplier Part Number: _____
- Supplier Drawing Number: _____ Revision Date: _____
- Certifications (Where Required): _____ Renewal Date: _____
- Material Certification Number: _____ MFG Date: _____

SUPPLIER INFORMATION:
- Business Name: _____ Supplier Code: _____
- Street Address: _____ Location/Division: _____
- City/State/Zip: _____ Sourcing Manager: _____
- Contact Name: _____ Other: _____

Original Manufacturer Information:
- Factory Name: _____ Vendor Code: _____
- Street Address: _____ Location/Division: _____
- City/State/Zip: _____ Sourcing Manager: _____
- Contact Name: _____ Other: _____

SUPPLIER STATUS:
Is the Supplier New or Existing? ☐ NEW ☐ Existing
If NEW, has the Supplier Selection & Approval process been initiated? ☐ YES ☐ NO

REASON FOR SUBMISSION: (CHECK ONE)
- ☐ New Component / Initial Submission
- ☐ New Supplier for Existing Component
- ☐ Supplier initiated changes that affect Form, Fit, or Function
- ☐ Existing component that has NOT been purchased for over 2 years
- ☐ OTHER: Please Specify Reason(s) Below
- ☐ Engineering Change
- ☐ Tooling: Transfer, Replacement, Refurbishment or Additional
- ☐ Change to Optional Construction or Material
- ☐ Part Produced at Additional Location
- ☐ Sub-Supplier or Material Source Change

Reason(s): _____

VENDOR REQUESTED SUBMITTAL: (CHECK ONE)
- ☐ Level 1 - Part Submission Warrant(PSW)
- ☐ Level 2 - Part Submission Warrant(PSW) with Product Samples and Limited Supporting Data
- ☐ Level 3 - Part Submission Warrant(PSW) with Product Samples and Complete Supporting Data
- ☐ Level 4 - Part Submission Warrant(PSW) and Other Special Requirements as Defined
- ☐ Level 5 - Visit Manufacturing Location for Audit / Inspection: This includes everything within submission levels 1 thru 4

**All Samples Submitted must be Tagged and Identified Appropriately. Please Print and Attach Included Shipping Label **

** Prior to PPAP submittal, all Critical To Quality (CtQ's) must meet or exceed a Process Capability Index (CpK) of 1.33 and ALL dimensions (including dimensions not identified as critical to quality) must fall within specifications drawing. **

DECLARATION: I hereby affirm that the samples represented by this warrant are representative of standard production and that all submission results meet requirements as well as all other appplicable regulatory standards and specifications.

- Print Name: _____ Phone: _____ Fax: _____
- Authorized Signature: _____ e-Mail: _____
- Title: _____ Date: _____

PPAP Approval Signature: _____ Date: _____

NOTIFICATION OF APPROVAL OR REJECTION WILL BE PROVIDED TO YOU BY PROCUREMENT OR PURCHASING.

Illustration 1-1

ISO 9001 & PPAP - Rethinking Solutions

The PPAP Cover Sheet you just completed has five warrant levels. Each warrant level will require some or all of the 18 PPAP checklist elements to be marked on this next form (*See Illustration 2-1*), This will guide what the supplier is actually required to complete and return for PPAP approval.

Our sample PPAP Checklist form (*See Illustration 2-1*) has fill in the blanks, laid out as follows for your reference:

KEY NOTE: This information should match the PPAP Cover Sheet and you should formulate a menu to auto populate spreadsheet cells to save duplicate data entry and time.

- ✓ PPAP # [This will be the next sequential number you pick from a custom PPAP sequential number spreadsheet log] If you don't have a sequential number log, create one inside your favorite spreadsheet software to prevent duplicate PPAP Numbers.]

- ✓ PURCHASE ORDER NUMBER: [This gets completed last, after the Supplier quality manager approves PPAP]

- ✓ REQUESTOR: [This is the Project manager's Name]

- ✓ TYPE OF PPAP - CHECK BOXES: [Select One]
    - o NEW PRODUCT?
    - o ENGINEERING CHANGE?
    - o SUPPLIER INITIATED CHANGE?
    - o OTHER?

ISO 9001 & PPAP - Rethinking Solutions

- ✓ PART NAME: [See your engineering's drawing and enter the Part Name]

- ✓ PART NUMBER: [See your engineering's drawing and enter the Part Number]

- ✓ DRAWING NUMBER: [See your engineering's drawing and enter the Drawing Number]

- ✓ DRAWING REVISION DATE: [See your engineering's drawing and enter the Drawings Revision Date]

KEY NOTE: If for some reason, your engineering department does not have a drawing, take the entire supplier's drawing with title block and tolerances and do a screen clip and then cut and paste this on to your title block with a disclaimer that supplier's title block supersedes your company's title block. Save with your new drawing number and your part number. This will give you a quick drawing and keep all the risk on the supplier's drawing.

- ✓ SUPPLIER PART NAME: [See supplier's drawing and enter the Supplier Part Name]

- ✓ SUPPLIER PART NUMBER: [See supplier's drawing and enter the Supplier Part Number]

- ✓ SUPPLIER DRAWING NUMBER: [See supplier's drawing and enter the Supplier Drawing Number]

ISO 9001 & PPAP - Rethinking Solutions

- ✓ SUPPLIER DRAWING REVISION DATE: [See supplier's drawing and enter the Supplier Drawings Revision Date]

- ✓ REASON FOR SUBMISSION - CHECK BOXES: [Select One]
    - o New Component / Initial Submission
    - o New Supplier for Existing Component
    - o Supplier initiated changes that affect Form, Fit or Function
    - o Existing component that has NOT been purchased for + 2 years
    - o Engineering Change
    - o Tooling: Transfer, Replacement, Refurbishment or Additional
    - o Change to Optional Construction or Material
    - o Part Produced at Additional Location
    - o Sub-Supplier or Material Source Change
    - o OTHER: Please Specify Reason(s) Below
        - ▪ REASON(S) = [Data Entry Lines]

- ✓ INSTRUCTIONS: [Never hurts to help others learn and assuring you get what you require]

    - o The PPAP Package is required to be submitted by the supplier with applicable product samples.
    - o The Supplier is required to provide completed documentation and data listed on the PPAP checklist below.
    - o Any Item checked in the checklist below is required for completion of the qualification of the part.

- o Any request for deviation from this requirement must be documented.
- o Data, photos and documentation is to be inserted into the worksheets labeled in this package.
- o Dimensional data provided in this documentation must be taken from the supplier's samples.
- o All material certifications must be provided for the material used to manufacture the samples.
- o Capability studies must be provided on all dimensions determined to be Critical to Quality (CtQ's) on the drawing.
- o All inspection equipment used in inspection of the product must be calibrated and/or certified.

✓ COMPLETE THE PPAP ITEMS CHECKED BELOW: [This will come from the PPAP Level 1 thru 5 you selected previously]

- o Remember PPAP is comprised of 18 key elements. I will list these below, while summarizing the key evidence criteria and my auditor notes.

KEY NOTE: You should create multiple color code tabs within your spreadsheet and provide instructions to help assure the supplier gives you the evidence you require.

ISO 9001 & PPAP - Rethinking Solutions

1.) **Design Documentation:**
   a. Customer Drawing
   b. Supplier's Drawing
   c. Purchase Order

KEY NOTE: Auditor shall verify the two drawings match and that all critical characteristics are agreed upon with signatures. The Purchase Order is required to ensure the correct part is being ordered at the correct revision.

2.) **Engineering Change Documents:**
   a. IF a PPAP is being completed due to a request for change to a product?
      i. ECN Documentation Requesting and approving the change
      ii. Revised Customer Drawing
      iii. Revised Supplier's Drawing
      iv. Representative's Purchase Order

KEY NOTE: Auditor shall verify the ECN, verify two drawings match and that all critical characteristics are agreed upon with signatures. The Purchase Order is required to ensure the correct part is being ordered at the correct revision.

3.) **Engineering Approval:**
   a. During the development process pre-PPAP samples are ordered for production intent
      i. Supplier's may send a waiver before testing can begin, otherwise:
         1. Engineers must test and approve Fit, Form, Function
         2. Engineers must complete an approval form

KEY NOTE: Auditor shall verify Engineer's approval form has signatures and if a waiver exists.

4.) **Design Failure Mode Effect Analysis (DFMEA):**
   a. DFMEA is a living document that is created during the design, testing and development process
      i. Typical DFMEA steps:
         - Review Design
         - Brainstorm Potential Failures
         - List potential effects of failure
         - Assign Severity rankings of failures
         - Assign Occurrence rankings of failures
         - Assign Detection rankings of failures
         - Calculate Risk Priority Number (RPN): Severity x Occurrence x Detection
         - Develop Action Plan
         - Take Action
         - Calculate Final (RPN): Multiply Severity x Occurrence x Detection

KEY NOTE: Auditor shall verify Engineer's DFMEA forms and Corrective Actions, IF included in the PPAP

5.) **Process Flow Diagram:**
   a. A flowchart diagram of the entire process for assembling the component to final assembly.
      i. A flowchart form that includes incoming material, assembly, testing, rework, etc. and shipping.

KEY NOTE: Auditor shall verify document

ISO 9001 & PPAP - Rethinking Solutions

6.) **Process Failure Mode Effect Analysis (PFMEA):**
    a. PFMEA is a living document that is created during the production process
        i. PFMEA looks at all areas of production & testing process to identify any potential quality issues:
            1. This document should be updated even after the product is released for production to allow for any issues that might come about during high volume assembly.

KEY NOTE: Auditor shall verify all PFMEA forms and Corrective Actions, IF included in the PPAP

7.) **Control Plan:**
    a. The Control Plan is based on the results of the PFMEA
        i. Includes the specific steps required to ensure that quality issues identified in the PFMEA will not be present in the final product.
        ii. Includes inline testing, quality inspections, incoming and outgoing quality processes.

KEY NOTE: Auditor shall compare verify Control Plan vs PFMEA evidence forms, IF included in the PPAP

8.) **Measurement System Analysis (MSA):**
    a. Gauge, Repeatability & Reproducibility studies on measurement equipment that is used during assembly or quality control checks to ensure repeatability of use does not diminish their accuracy
    b. Calibration stickers and schedules should also be reviewed

KEY NOTE: Auditor shall verify all measurement documentation

9.) Dimensional Analysis:
   a. When the production line has completed the production validation, samples from these builds are used to complete dimensional inspections. Every ballooned dimension on the drawings is measured to make sure it falls within specifications and compiled on a spreadsheet

KEY NOTE: Auditor shall verify all measurement documentation

10.) Initial Sample Inspection Report:
   a. A sample report completed prior to building the first prototypes
      i. This report will verify that the incoming parts meet specifications and are ready for prototype assembly

KEY NOTE: Auditor shall verify all documentation & dimensions

11.) Initial Process Studies:
   a. Initial process studies will be done on all the production processes and will include Statistical Process Control (SPC) charts on the critical characteristics of the product. These studies demonstrate that the critical processes are stable and are ready to begin the process validation builds.

KEY NOTE: Auditor shall verify quality documentation and processes at the supplier's facilities

12.) Qualified Laboratory Documentation:
   a. Qualified laboratory documentation includes all of the industry certifications for ANY lab that was involved in completing validation testing.

KEY NOTE: Auditor shall verify documents or photos of documents exist within PPAP

ISO 9001 & PPAP - Rethinking Solutions

13.) <u>Appearance Approval Report (AAR)</u>:
    a. The AAR is a report that verifies that the customer has inspected the final product and it meets all the required appearance specifications for the design.
    b. Report will include Color, Textures, Fit Gaps between Parts, Etc.

KEY NOTE: Auditor shall verify documents or photos of documents exist within PPAP

14.) <u>Sample Production Parts</u>:
    a. Sample production parts are sent to customer for approval
        i. Parts are stored for Active production, plus one year
        ii. Electronic PPAP files are stored a lifetime and should include photos of sample parts along with the physical location that the parts are stored

KEY NOTE: Auditor shall verify sample parts match documents that exist within PPAP

15.) <u>Master Sample</u>:
    a. A master sample needs to be identified, labeled and signed off

KEY NOTE: Auditor shall verify master sample and label

16.) <u>Checking Aids</u>:
    a. Checking aids are used by production and are a detailed list of all the tools used to inspect, test, or measure parts during the assembly process.
        i. Each aid will list the part, describe the tool and have the calibration schedule for the tool

KEY NOTE: Auditor shall verify Checking Aids & documents

ISO 9001 & PPAP - Rethinking Solutions

17.) <u>Records Material / Performance Tests:</u>
   a. This is the largest section of the PPAP and includes all the product validation and certification testing that was completed on the product. These documents demonstrate the product meets all specifications.

KEY NOTE: Auditor shall verify all documentation

18.) Part Submission Warrant (PSW):
   a. This is the final document that is included in the PPAP package
   b. This form is a summary of the entire PPAP submission and specifies
      i. Drawing Number & Revisions
      ii. Deviations covered by the PPAP submission
      iii. Customer Sign-off

KEY NOTE: Auditor shall verify all documents

✓ NUMBER OF PPAP SAMPLES SUBMITTED = [Enter the number of PPAP Samples required]

- I have found for smaller industries that a request for 5 samples will work for parts with non-critical dimensions or a color change.
- I request 30 samples for parts with critical dimensions
- If a part cannot be easily produced for a color change scenario, then 5 color chips are acceptable.

KEY NOTE: If a part cannot be easily produced as requested for PPAP samples, then a purchasing agreement / amendment must be signed, stating the Supplier assumes all risks if the Supplier quality manager rejects

- ✓ DISCLAIMERS: [Add your special requirements here]

    - o All samples submitted must be tagged and identified appropriately. Please print and attach our provided shipping label.
    - o Prior to PPAP submittal, all Critical to Quality (CtQ's) must meet or exceed a Process Capability Index (CpK) of 1.33 and ALL dimensions (including dimensions not identified as critical to quality) must fall within specifications of drawing.

- ✓ DECLARATION = [Fill in blanks as required]
    - o LEGAL STATEMENT: [I hereby affirm that the samples represented by this warrant are representative of standard production and that all submission meet requirements as well as all other applicable regulatory standards and specifications.]

KEY NOTE: In the automotive world, PPAP's can cost a lot of money for traveling, RUN at RATE verifications, etc. and are most likely negotiated inside the purchase order, however, when you don't have the budget to dive that deep, but you want the security of PPAP, then you have to address and input these types of legal statements. I would also tighten the belt on your ISO Supplier Risk Assessments.

- NAME: [Supplier's Contact Name]
- TITLE: [Supplier's Company Title]
- PHONE: [Supplier's Phone]
- FAX: [Supplier's Fax]
- E-MAIL: [Supplier's E-mail]
- DATE: [Date Supplier Signed]
- AUTHORIZED SIGNATURE: [This is the authorized supplier's signature, required to get the PPAP process started]

✓ Don't forget to make this a controlled document with a revision date

Congratulations you just completed a PPAP Submission Checklist with instructions on how to create your entire PPAP warrant package.

ISO 9001 & PPAP - Rethinking Solutions

Production Part Approval Process (PPAP) Checklist

PPAP #:	Purchase Order Number:	REQUESTOR:
☐ NEW PRODUCT	☐ ENGINEERING CHANGE ☐ SUPPLIER INITIATED CHANGE	☐ OTHER

PART INFORMATION:

- Part Name: _____
- Part Number: _____
- Drawing Number: _____ Revision Date: _____
- Supplier Part Name: _____
- Supplier Part Number: _____
- Supplier Drawing Number: _____ Revision Date: _____

REASON FOR SUBMISSION: (CHECK ONE)

- ☐ New Component / Initial Submission
- ☐ New Supplier for Existing Component
- ☐ Supplier initiated changes that affect Form, Fit, or Function
- ☐ Existing component that has NOT been purchased for over 2 years
- ☐ OTHER: Please Specify Reason(s) Below
- ☐ Engineering Change
- ☐ Tooling: Transfer, Replacement, Refurbishment or Additional
- ☐ Change to Optional Construction or Material
- ☐ Part Produced at Additional Location
- ☐ Sub-Supplier or Material Source Change

Reason(s): _____

INSTRUCTIONS:

* The PPAP Package is required to be submitted by the supplier with applicable product samples.
* The Supplier is required to provide completed documentation and data listed on the PPAP checklist below.
* Any item checked in the checklist below is required for completion of the qualification of the part.
* Any request for deviation from this requirement must be documented.
* Data, photos and documentation is to be inserted into the worksheets labeled in this package.
* Dimensional data provided in this documentation must be taken from the supplied samples
* All material certifications must be provided for the material used to manufacture the samples.
* Capability studies must be provided on all dimensions determined to be Critical To Quality(CTQs) on the drawing.
* All inspection equipment used in inspection of the product must be calibrated and/or certified.

COMPLETE THE PPAP ITEMS CHECKED BELOW:

- ☐ 1.) Design Documentation
- ☐ 2.) Engineering Change Documents
- ☐ 3.) Engineering Approval
- ☐ 4.) Design Failure Mode Effect Analysis (DFMEA)
- ☐ 5.) Process Flow Diagram
- ☐ 6.) Process Failure Mode Effect Analysis (PFMEA)
- ☐ 7.) Control Plan
- ☐ 8.) Measurement System Analysis (MSA)
- ☐ 9.) Dimensional Analysis
- ☐ 10.) Initial Sample Inspection Report
- ☐ 11.) Initial Process Studies
- ☐ 12.) Qualified Laboratory Documentation
- ☐ 13.) Appearance Approval Report (AAR)
- ☐ 14.) Sample Production Parts
- ☐ 15.) Master Sample
- ☐ 16.) Checking Aids
- ☐ 17.) Records Material / Performance Tests
- ☐ 18.) Part Submission Warrant (PSW)

Number of PPAP Samples Submitted = _____   Total Number of PPAP Samples Run @ Rate = _____

All Samples Submitted must be Tagged and Identified Appropriately. Please Print and Attach Included Shipping Label

** Prior to PPAP submittal, all Critical To Quality (CtQ's) must meet or exceed a Process Capability Index (CpK) of 1.33 and ALL dimensions (including dimensions not identified as critical to quality) must fall within specifications of drawing. **

DECLARATION: I hereby affirm that the samples represented by this warrant are representative of standard production and that all submission results meet requirements as well as all other appplicable regulatory standards and specifications.

- Print Name: _____ Phone: _____ Fax: _____
- Authorized Signature: _____ e-Mail: _____
- Title: _____ Date: _____

Illustration 2-1

ISO 9001 & PPAP - Rethinking Solutions

Receiving Quality Materials

PPAP is now approved and the parts are being delivered. But wait, we are not finished, receiving quality materials is equally important.

- ✓ Quality production starts with receiving defect-free parts that measure to print and are within design specifications. Track the shipment!

- ✓ All incoming materials must pass quality inspections and be tagged "approved for production", before being received into inventory.

    KEY NOTE: Crosstrain forklift drivers to do quality inspections, since they already handle the materials the most. Plus, they are already a skilled resource and know the inventory layout and part numbers. Even if a quality finding is questionable, they can easily contact the Supplier quality manager for assistance.

- ✓ Larger materials should be inspected on the semi-trailers, before unloading. When you reject a few loads like this at the docks, you force the driver and the supplier to train to contain and not waste deliveries.

    KEY NOTE: Garbage in, garbage out. Do everything you can to not let bad supplied materials infect your quality manufactured products.

Supplier Corrective Action Request (SCAR)

Everything passed PPAP, but a few months later the supplied product is nonconforming and is causing much chaos, including missed shipments.

This section will be a brief overview, because we have all been down this path, with or without ISO 9001. Quarantine and tag the nonconforming materials (NCM), complete your NCM forms, capture photos of everything including the shipping labels with the lot numbers and serial numbers, etc. for traceability. Next make sure the cost recovery section on this form is completed and approved by your plant manager before sending this completed NCM paper work to the supplier quality manager. The supplier quality manager will contact the material planners to have them to assist with RMA numbers and inventory levels to keep production moving while issuing the SCAR.

The SCAR is a Supplier Corrective Action Request. You are requesting the supplier to do a formal root cause investigation and then document everything on how they will prevent this defect from happening again. This formal document provided to you will need to be reviewed and approved, because you cannot accept excuses like "the normal operator was on vacation…" The SCAR process will force suppliers to train to contain as there could be huge financial cost recovery penalties involved.

KEY NOTE: If suppliers complain about the cost recovery, remind them that they agreed to PPAP, so pay the bill and don't send us your problems.

Conclusion

This book and its content is not a replacement for the complete information found at www.ISO.org, www.OSHA.gov, www.NFPA.org, www.AIAG.org

The information in this book is distributed "AS IS", without warranty.

This work is copyrighted © 2017. All rights reserved. No part of this publication may be reproduced or distributed in any form without the prior written permission from JUSTRETHINK, LLC.

Hopefully the unique teaching mechanisms inside this book will help you to Just Rethink the values of:

- ✓ Employee Satisfaction
- ✓ Safety
- ✓ Supplier Quality
- ✓ ISO 9001:2015
- ✓ Production Part Approval Process (PPAP)
- ✓ Receiving Quality & SCARS

The Just Rethinking Solution information and notes provided should be an excellent reference guide to help you create your own PPAP integrated ISO 9001 system. Stay tuned… more Just Rethink Solutions are on the way.

Thank You!

ISO 9001 & PPAP - Rethinking Solutions

ISO 9001 & PPAP - Rethinking Solutions

Review Questions

1.) **What is Rethinking?**

Answer is on page #6

2.) **What does PPAP stand for?**

Answer is on page #6

3.) **What was the challenge?**

Answer is on page #7 - 9

4.) **What do Quality Auditors do very well?**

Answer is on page #10

5.) **Satisfied Employees, do what?**

Answer is on page #13

6.) **By law, what does OSHA require?**

Answer is on page #14

7.) **What does the PPAP process ensures?**

Answer is on page #21

Index

A

action, 5,9
advanced, 4,9
advise, 8
alert, 8
Amortization, 6
Analyst, 4
Android, 4
APPs, 4
Assessment, 5
assessment, 6
Auditing, 7
auditors, 10
author, 3
authority, 10
Automation, 4
automotive, 4,9

B

barriers, 8

Black Belt, 6

blunt, 10
boss, 9
BS, 7

C

Calibration, 8
CEO, 4
certifications, 4
challenge, 7, 9
challenges, 7
change, 6, 10
changes, 10
chaos, 8
chart, 10
clueless, 7
Conclusion, 5
consultant, 8
consulting, 4
Contents, 5
control, 9
copyrighted, 3
Corrective, 5, 9
credentials, 6

D

Data, 8
data, 7
defects, 6
Deja vu, 7
Depreciation, 6
drama, 9

E

earn, 8
Earnings, 6
EBITDA, 6

elite, 6

Email, 4
Employee, 5, 6, 9

employment, 9

encourage, 10
Engineering, 4, 8
English, 6, 8
Equipment, 7, 8
evaluations, 8
example, 4, 7, 9
experience, 4, 6
expert, 6
expertise, 4
experts, 7

F

factory, 7

failing, 6
failure, 6

fault, 10

fear, 10
find, 7, 10
finding, 3

G

garbage, 9
Gear, 7

H

help, 6, 8, 9

I

incomplete, 7
industries, 7
industry, 4
info, 4
instructions, 7
integrate, 6
Introduction, 5, 6
ISO, 5, 7, 9
IT, 4

J

job, 6
jobs, 10
JUSTRETHINK, 4, 6

K

knowledge, 8

L

Language, 8
Lead, 9
Leadership, 7
LEAN, 7, 8
leather, 7
listening, 8

LLC, 4, 6

M

magic, 7
Maintenance, 7
Management, 4, 7, 9
management, 6, 9
manager, 8
managers, 8
managing, 6
Manufacturing, 4, 6, 7
Materials, 5
Matrix, 8
McVay, 4
mechanisms, 4, 9
meetings, 7
Merge, 5
MSDS, 8

N

Negativity, 9

O

Operator, 8
Operators, 8
opportunities, 9
organizational, 10
OSHA, 5

P

packaging, 7
people, 6, 8, 10
permission, 3
Personal, 7
pharmaceutical, 7
Phone, 4
Plan, 5, 10
plant, 8
PM, 7
Poka-Yoke, 8
Poor, 6, 8
PPAP, 5, 6, 9
PPE, 7
practice, 8
Preventative, 7
problems, 4, 6
products, 7
professionals, 7

Programming, 4
protected, 7
Protective, 7

Q

QMS, 9
Quality, 4, 5, 7, 10
question, 8
quit, 7

R

rates, 8

receiving, 5
recognition, 8
records, 7
reorganize, 9
reproduced, 3
request, 5
resume, 10
Robotics, 4

S

safety, 4, 5, 8
satisfied, 6, 7, 9
SCAR, 5
SCARs, 9
shortcomings, 6
sigma, 6, 7
solution, 4
solutions, 4
solver, 4

supervisor, 8
supervisors, 8
Supplier, 5, 9
suppliers, 4, 6
surveys, 8
Synergy, 5

T

Taxes, 6
team, 7, 9
Technology, 8
tier, 4
tolerances, 8
tools, 7
Training, 8
Tribal, 8
trust, 8

truth, 10
TS 16949, 6

U

unannounced, 8
unit, 7

V

verify, 7
Violations, 8

W

Why, 6, 9
work, 3, 7, 9, 10
Workstations, 8
world, 4
WWII, 6

Y

Yoke, 8

If your ISO 9001 QMS is failing to keep your best employees, customers and EBITDA's (Earnings Before Interest, Taxes, Depreciation and Amortization) satisfied, then none of your credentials matter and you need to Just Rethink for the next hour. Good news! Just Rethink, LLC can help. Our Just Rethinking Solutions books are designed to be less than a one hour read and will help you navigate through pitfalls and possible points of failures, while teaching you how to merge in PPAP (Production Part Approval Process) to find the key to successful Supplier Quality Management which stops garbage in, garbage out, so you can worry less and get your production back on track. Just Rethink and purchase today!

Printed in Great Britain
by Amazon